The Gift of Godly Friendship

A Bible Study for Women Who Long for Meaningful Connection

DR. LENDE CLICK

The Gift of Godly Friendship

A Bible Study for Women Who Long for Meaningful Connection

Copyright © 2026 by **Lende Click**

All rights reserved.

No part of this book may be reproduced, stored in a retrieval system, or transmitted in any form or by any means—electronic, mechanical, photocopying, recording, or otherwise—without prior written permission from the author, except for brief quotations used in reviews.

Scripture quotations are taken from the **King James Version (KJV)** of the Bible.

This book is for inspirational and devotional purposes only.

Published by **Lende Click Publishing**

Author: Dr. **Lende Click**
Cover Design: Dr. **Lende Click**
Interior Design: Dr. **Lende Click**

Printed in the United States of America

Dedication

This book is dedicated
to every woman whose heart has ever quietly whispered
for meaningful connection,
faithful friendship,
and the comfort of being truly known.

To the woman who has rejoiced in the gift of true
companionship,
and to the woman who has wept through seasons
of loneliness, disappointment, or unseen sorrow—
may these words rest gently upon your heart.

May the God who formed you for love and fellowship
heal every place wounded by rejection,
restore every place wearied by loss,
and lead you into the beauty of Christ-centered friendship.

May He teach you that your longing is not weakness,
but part of His tender design—
and may you find in Him
the faithful foundation of every friendship
your heart has ever desired.

For the One who created you for connection
is also the One who holds your heart with perfect love.

Table of Contents

Introduction

Friendship is one of God's sweetest gifts.

From the beginning, the Lord showed us that we were not created to walk through life alone. He made us for fellowship, encouragement, love, and support. He made us with a longing for meaningful connection—a desire to be known, understood, strengthened, and cared for. Yet for many women, friendship can also be a place of deep longing, disappointment, loneliness, and even pain.

Some women have been blessed with faithful friends who have stood beside them through many seasons. Others have known the heartache of being misunderstood, left out, betrayed, or forgotten. Some carry silent wounds from broken friendships. Some desire deeper connection but do not know where to begin. And some have learned to guard their hearts because of what they have walked through.

But even in all of this, God has not left us without hope.

His Word shows us what true friendship looks like. It teaches us how to love well, how to walk in wisdom, how to encourage one another, how to heal from relational pain, and how to build relationships that honor Him. Most of all, Scripture reminds us that the foundation of every healthy friendship begins with the Lord Himself. As we draw closer to God, He teaches us how to become the kind of women who reflect His love, His grace, His truth, and His faithfulness in our relationships.

The Gift of Godly Friendship was written for the woman who longs for meaningful connection. It is for the woman who desires Christ-centered friendship. It is for the woman who wants to grow in wisdom, love, discernment, and grace. It is for the woman who has been hurt in friendship and needs healing. And it is for the woman who wants to become a godly friend herself.

Over these next twelve weeks, we will walk through what the Bible says about connection, loyalty, encouragement, wisdom, forgiveness, healing, boundaries, sisterhood, and lasting friendship. Each week is designed to help you not only understand biblical friendship more deeply, but also to invite God into your own heart, relationships, and desires.

This study is not just about finding the right friends. It is also about becoming the right friend. It is about allowing God to shape your heart so that your friendships reflect His beauty and His truth. It is about learning that meaningful connection is not built merely on common interests or shared moments, but on love that is rooted in Christ.

As you begin this journey, I pray you will find comfort for the lonely places, healing for the wounded places, wisdom for the guarded places, and hope for the places that still long for godly friendship. I pray you will discover that the Lord sees your heart, understands your desire for connection, and is able to bring beautiful, life-giving relationships into your life in His perfect way and timing.

May this study draw you closer to the heart of God and teach you the beauty of walking with others in faith, love, and truth.

Key Scripture

Ecclesiastes 4:9–10
"Two are better than one, because they have a good reward for their labor. For if they fall, the one will lift up his fellow. But woe to him that is alone when he falleth, for he hath not another to help him up."

Week 1:

God Created Us for Connection

Theme

We were never meant to walk through life alone.

Opening Thought

From the very beginning, God showed that human beings were created for relationship. Before sin entered the world, before pain and brokenness touched the human heart, the Lord looked at Adam and said, **"It is not good that the man should be alone"** (Genesis 2:18). This was not only about marriage—it also reveals something deeper about the heart of God. The Lord created us with a need for connection, companionship, encouragement, and fellowship.

Women especially often carry a deep desire to be known, loved, understood, and supported. God placed that longing in the heart. Wanting meaningful friendship is not weakness. It is part of how God designed us. He never intended for us to carry every burden alone, fight every battle alone, or walk through every season without encouragement.

In a world where many women feel lonely, overlooked, rejected, or disconnected, the Word of God reminds us that we were made for more. We were created for relationship with God first, and then for healthy, life-giving connection with others. Friendship, fellowship, and sisterhood are gifts from the Lord.

Godly connection strengthens us. It gives comfort in sorrow, encouragement in weariness, wisdom in confusion, and joy in the journey. The enemy often tries to isolate women through fear, insecurity, pain, and disappointment, because isolation makes the heart feel heavy and vulnerable. But God's design is not isolation. His design is loving, wise, healthy connection.

When we understand that God created us for connection, we stop seeing our longing for meaningful friendship as something to hide or be ashamed of. Instead, we begin to see it as part of God's beautiful design. He made us to walk with Him and to encourage one another along the way.

Key Scriptures

Genesis 2:18
"And the Lord God said, "It is not good that the man should be alone; I will make him a helper meet for him."

Ecclesiastes 4:9–10
"Two are better than one, because they have a good reward for their labor. For if they fall, the one will lift up his fellow. But woe to him that is alone when he falleth, for he hath not another to help him up."

Hebrews 10:24–25

"And let us consider one another to provoke unto love and to good works, not forsaking the assembling of ourselves together, as is the manner of some, but exhorting one another, and so much the more as ye see the Day approaching."

Lesson

Connection is part of God's design.

Many women feel guilty for longing for close friendships. Some have been hurt so deeply that they try to convince themselves they do not need anyone. Others feel embarrassed by their loneliness, as though needing friendship means they are weak or immature. But the truth is, God made us with a desire for fellowship.

Throughout Scripture, we see the beauty of godly connection. Ruth stayed with Naomi in loyalty. David and Jonathan shared deep covenant friendship. The early church gathered together, prayed together, encouraged one another, and carried one another's burdens. The Bible does not present faith as a journey we were meant to walk alone.

This does not mean every relationship will be safe or every friendship will be deep. It does mean that the desire for meaningful connection is not wrong. It is God-given. The problem is not the longing itself. The problem comes when we look for fulfillment in unhealthy places, or when pain causes us to shut down completely.

God wants to heal our view of friendship. He wants us to understand that meaningful connection begins with Him. As we grow in our relationship with the Lord, He teaches us how to build relationships that are wise, healthy, loving, and honoring to Him.

Sometimes the deepest loneliness is not caused by being physically alone, but by feeling unseen, misunderstood, or unsupported. Yet God sees every hidden ache. He knows every disappointment, every silent tear, and every longing for a faithful friend. He cares about the relational needs of your heart.

The Lord does not shame your longing for connection. He understands it, because He created you with it. And when your heart feels lonely, He invites you not into despair, but into His presence. He also teaches you how to pursue meaningful connection in ways that are grounded in truth, wisdom, and grace.

Healthy friendship is not about having a large number of people around you. It is about having relationships marked by sincerity, faithfulness, encouragement, and love. Even one godly, trustworthy friendship can be a great blessing. God knows how to bring the right people into your life in the right season.

Week 1 is a reminder that you were not created to live emotionally shut down, spiritually isolated, or relationally hopeless. You were created by a loving God who understands your need for connection and who is able to meet you in that longing.

Reflection Questions

1. Have you ever felt lonely even when surrounded by people?

____

____

____

2. How does it make you feel to know that God created you for connection?

____

____

____

3. Have past wounds ever made you want to pull away from friendship?

____

____

____

4. In what ways have you seen isolation affect your heart or spiritual life?

____

____

____

5. What kind of meaningful connection are you longing for in this season?

____

____

____

6. How can you begin inviting God into that longing?

____

____

____

7. What does healthy, godly friendship look like to you?

____

____

____

Prayer

Lord, thank You for creating me with a heart that longs for love, fellowship, and meaningful connection. Help me to understand that this desire is not weakness, but part of how You made me. Heal every place in me that has been wounded by loneliness, rejection, or broken friendship. Draw me closer to You, and teach me how to build healthy, godly relationships. Protect me from isolation, discouragement, and fear. Help me to trust that You know the needs of my heart and that You are able to bring the right people into my life in Your perfect time. In Jesus' name, Amen.

Closing Encouragement

Your longing for meaningful connection does not make you needy—it makes you human. God sees your heart, understands your desire, and cares about every lonely place within you. You were created by a loving God who made you for relationship, encouragement, and fellowship. You are not forgotten, and you are not meant to walk alone.

Week 2:

Friendship Begins with God

Theme

The foundation of every healthy friendship is our relationship with the Lord.

Opening Thought

Before we can build strong and meaningful friendships with others, we must first understand the beauty of friendship with God. Human friendships can be a blessing, but no earthly relationship can fill the deepest places of the heart the way the Lord can. When our hearts are rooted in Him, we learn how to love others in a healthier, wiser, and more godly way.

Many women long for faithful friendship, yet sometimes they look to people to give what only God can give—complete security, perfect understanding, constant peace, and unfailing love. People may care deeply, but they are still human. They may fail, disappoint, misunderstand, or fall short. Only the Lord is perfectly faithful.

Friendship with God changes us. It teaches us trust, faithfulness, love, humility, grace, and truth. It heals the empty places that often cause us to cling too tightly to others or feel crushed when human relationships do not meet every longing. The closer we grow to the Lord, the more we discover that He is not distant. He is near, personal, loving, and deeply involved in our lives.

Jesus called His followers friends. What a beautiful truth. The holy Son of God invites us into closeness with Him—not because we deserve it, but because of His love and grace. When friendship begins with God, we are no longer building our relationships on fear, desperation, insecurity, or emotional emptiness. Instead, we are building from a place of being loved, known, and anchored in Christ.

Key Scriptures

John 15:13–15
"Greater love hath no man than this, that a man lay down his life for his friends. Ye are my friends, if ye do whatsoever I command you. Henceforth I call you not servants; for the servant knoweth not what his lord doeth: but I have called you friends; for all things that I have heard of my Father I have made known unto you."

James 2:23
"And the scripture was fulfilled which saith, Abraham believed God, and it was imputed unto him for righteousness: and he was called the Friend of God."

Psalm 25:14

"The secret of the Lord is with them that fear Him, and He will show them His covenant."

Lesson

True friendship begins with God.

Many women spend years searching for connection, understanding, and emotional safety in human relationships, yet still feel empty inside. That is because the deepest need of the heart is not first for human friendship, but for communion with God. We were made by Him, and we were made for Him.

When our relationship with the Lord becomes the center of our lives, it changes the way we view friendship. We stop expecting people to be our savior. We stop placing impossible weight on human relationships. We stop looking for others to complete what only God can heal. Instead, we learn to receive from the Lord first.

Jesus gives us the perfect picture of friendship. He loved sacrificially. He spoke truth. He showed compassion. He remained faithful. He laid down His life. His love was not shallow, selfish, or temporary. It was holy, steadfast, and full of grace. The more we abide in Him, the more His character begins to shape the way we treat others.

Friendship with God also gives discernment. When a woman is close to the Lord, she becomes more sensitive to what is healthy and what is not. She learns to recognize relationships that draw her nearer to God and those that pull her away from peace, wisdom, and truth. The presence of God becomes the place where her heart is grounded.

Sometimes friendship wounds run so deep that a woman becomes afraid to trust again. But friendship with God is a safe place for healing. He does not betray. He does not abandon. He does not mock your pain or overlook your tears. He listens, comforts, strengthens, and restores. In His presence, the heart begins to heal.

This does not mean human friendship is unimportant. It means human friendship is healthiest when it flows from a life rooted in God. When you know you are already loved by Him, you no longer approach friendship from constant fear of rejection. When you know He sees you, you no longer need people to validate your worth. When you know He is faithful, you learn how to love with wisdom rather than desperation.

God is not only the giver of friendship—He is the beginning of it. If we want godly connection, we must first learn to walk closely with Him. Friendship with God is the foundation upon which every other healthy relationship is built.

Reflection Questions

1. What does it mean to you that Jesus calls His followers friends?

____

____

____

2. Have you ever looked to people to give what only God can give?

____

____

____

3. In what ways has your relationship with God shaped your relationships with others?

____

____

____

4. Are there places in your heart that still need healing from disappointment or rejection?

____

____

____

5. How does friendship with God bring comfort to lonely places in your heart?

____

____

____

6. What would it look like for you to draw closer to God in this season?

____

____

____

7. How can a deeper walk with God help you become a healthier friend to others?

____

____

____

Prayer

Lord, thank You that You are not distant from me, but near to my heart. Thank You for loving me with a love that never fails. Help me to build my life on friendship with You first. Forgive me for the times I have looked to people to fill places that only You can fill. Heal every wounded place in my heart, and teach me to trust You more deeply. Draw me into closer fellowship with You, and let Your love shape the way I see myself and others. Help me to build friendships from a place of peace, wisdom, and security in You. In Jesus' name, Amen.

Closing Encouragement

The strongest friendships do not begin with people — they begin with God. When your heart is rooted in His love, you are no longer seeking friendship from emptiness, but from fullness in Him. The Lord is your faithful foundation, your safe place, and your truest Friend.

When you walk closely with God, He prepares your heart for healthy, meaningful, Christ-centered connection.

Week 3:

Becoming a Godly Friend

Theme

Before seeking a godly friend, we must first become one.

Opening Thought

Many women desire faithful, loving, and trustworthy friendships. They long for someone who will encourage them, pray for them, stand by them, and walk with them through life's joys and sorrows. These are beautiful desires. But as we seek meaningful connection, we must also ask an important question: **Am I becoming the kind of friend I am praying for?**

Godly friendship is not built only on finding the right people. It is also built on becoming the right kind of person. The Lord cares not only about the friends we choose, but also about the character we carry into our relationships. A godly friend is not perfect, but she is growing. She is learning to love with sincerity, speak with kindness, walk in humility, and remain faithful in truth and grace.

In a world where many relationships are shallow, self-centered, or inconsistent, God calls His daughters to a higher way. He calls us to be women who reflect His heart in the way we love others. A godly friend is a gift. She brings peace instead of confusion, encouragement instead of tearing down, and faithfulness instead of unreliability. She is not controlled by jealousy, pride, gossip, or selfishness. She is being shaped by the character of Christ.

Becoming a godly friend begins in the heart. It begins with allowing the Holy Spirit to teach us how to love people in a way that honors the Lord. When God forms our character, our friendships begin to carry His beauty.

Key Scriptures

Proverbs 17:17
"A friend loveth at all times, and a brother is born for adversity."

Colossians 3:12–14
"Put on therefore, as the elect of God, holy and beloved, bowels of mercies, kindness, humbleness of mind, meekness, longsuffering; Forbearing one another, and forgiving one another, if any man have a quarrel against any: even as Christ forgave you, so also do ye. And above all these things put on charity, which is the bond of perfectness."

Philippians 2:3–4
"Let nothing be done through strife or vainglory; but in lowliness of mind let each esteem other better than themselves. Look not every man on his own things, but every man also on the things of others."

Lesson

Godly friendship flows from godly character.

It is easy to focus on what we want from others. We may desire loyalty, honesty, kindness, and support. But Scripture teaches us to also examine our own hearts. Are we trustworthy? Are we kind with our words? Do we listen well? Do we make room for others, or do we only want to be understood ourselves? Do we pray for our friends, or do we only talk to them when we need something?

A godly friend loves at all times. This does not mean she never sets boundaries or never speaks truth. It means her love is steady, sincere, and rooted in Christ. She does not love only when it is convenient. She does not disappear when life gets hard. She understands that friendship requires faithfulness.

Kindness is a mark of godly friendship. A kind friend is careful with her words. She does not use her tongue to wound, embarrass, or belittle. She speaks with gentleness and wisdom. Her presence becomes a place of comfort rather than fear. In a world where words can be sharp and careless, kindness is a powerful reflection of Jesus.

Humility is also necessary in friendship. Pride makes relationships difficult. Pride must always be right, always be first, and always be seen. But humility makes space for love. It allows a woman to apologize, to listen, to forgive, and to care about the needs of others. A humble friend is teachable and gracious.

Faithfulness matters deeply. Many people know how to be friendly, but not everyone knows how to be faithful. A godly friend is dependable. She keeps confidence. She does not gossip. She does not betray private matters. She can be trusted. Her loyalty reflects the heart of God.

A godly friend also walks in grace. Every friendship will face misunderstandings, disappointments, and moments of weakness, because no one is perfect. Grace helps us be patient with one another. It helps us forgive, communicate honestly, and grow through challenges rather than walking away too quickly.

This does not mean we must strive to become flawless. It means we must surrender our hearts to the Lord and allow Him to shape us. Becoming a godly friend is part of spiritual maturity. As Christ works in us, we become women who carry His love into our relationships.

Sometimes the friendships we desire begin with the character we are willing to develop. God may be using this season not only to bring godly people into your life, but also to make you into a godly woman whose presence is safe, wise, faithful, and full of grace.

Reflection Questions

1. What kind of friend do you desire to have in your life?

____

____

____

2. Are those same qualities growing in your own heart?

____

____

____

3. In what areas do you feel the Lord is teaching you to become a better friend?

____

____

____

4. Are your words life-giving, gentle, and trustworthy?

____

____

____

5. Do you struggle more with pride, impatience, jealousy, hurt, or insecurity in friendships?

____

____

____

6. What does faithfulness in friendship look like in your life?

____

____

____

7. How can you reflect the love of Christ more clearly in your relationships?

____

____

____

Prayer

Lord, thank You for showing me through Your Word what godly friendship looks like. Help me not only to seek good friends, but also to become one. Shape my heart to reflect Your love, kindness, humility, and faithfulness. Forgive me for the times I have been impatient, self-focused, wounded, or careless in relationships. Teach me to speak with grace, listen with compassion, and love with sincerity. Make me into a woman whose friendships honor You. In Jesus' name, Amen.

Closing Encouragement

You do not have to be perfect to be a godly friend — you simply need a heart that is willing to be shaped by God. As He grows your character, He will teach you how to love with wisdom, walk in humility, and build friendships that reflect His heart.

The more you become like Christ, the more your friendships will carry His beauty.

Week 4:

Choosing Wise Friendships

Theme

Not every connection is a godly connection.

Opening Thought

Friendship is a gift from God, but not every friendship is meant to have deep access to your heart. One of the most important lessons a woman can learn is that while we are called to love everyone, we are not called to walk closely with everyone. Some relationships bring peace, encouragement, and spiritual strength. Others bring confusion, compromise, and pain.

Choosing wise friendships is not about being critical, proud, or judgmental. It is about walking in discernment. God wants His daughters to be loving, but He also wants them to be wise. A woman who lacks discernment may open her heart too quickly, trust too easily, and ignore warning signs that later bring sorrow. But a woman who walks with God learns that healthy friendship requires both love and wisdom.

Some friendships are built on shared faith, honesty, encouragement, and mutual respect. Others are built only on convenience, emotion, flattery, gossip, or unhealthy dependence. A godly friend will not draw you away from peace, purity, truth, or your walk with the Lord. Wise friendship should strengthen your spiritual life, not weaken it.

God cares deeply about the people we allow close to us. The voices we welcome, the company we keep, and the relationships we nurture all have influence. That is why Scripture teaches us to choose wisely. Not every open door is from God, and not every person who enters our life is meant to remain in a close place.

Key Scriptures

Proverbs 13:20
"He that walketh with wise men shall be wise: but a companion of fools shall be destroyed."

1 Corinthians 15:33
"Be not deceived: evil communications corrupt good manners."

Amos 3:3
"Can two walk together, except they be agreed?"

Lesson

Godly friendship requires discernment.

Many women have been hurt because they mistook closeness for safety. A person may seem kind at first, but not everyone carries the character needed for trustworthy friendship. Some people are drawn to your life for the wrong reasons. Some want access without accountability. Some enjoy your presence but do not honor your peace. This is why discernment is so important.

Choosing wise friendships begins with understanding that influence matters. The people closest to you can shape your thoughts, your attitudes, your habits, and even your spiritual direction. If a friendship constantly pulls you toward negativity, compromise, drama, gossip, or emotional exhaustion, it is not a healthy place for your heart. A wise friend should help you grow, not pull you down.

A godly friendship will carry certain fruit. It will have honesty, kindness, faithfulness, and respect. It will not pressure you to violate your convictions. It will not feed on jealousy, manipulation, competition, or constant chaos. Wise friendships make room for truth and grace. They bring peace, not confusion.

Discernment also means paying attention to patterns. Sometimes women ignore warning signs because they do not want to seem unkind, or because they deeply desire connection. But wisdom looks beyond words and notices fruit. Does this person keep confidence, or do they gossip? Do they honor boundaries, or do they push past them? Do they celebrate your growth, or do they compete with it? Do they respect your walk with God, or do they mock what matters to you?

Not every friendship must become a deep friendship. Some people belong in a casual place, not a close place. This is not rejection—it is wisdom. God never asked you to give everyone equal access to your heart. There are different levels of relationship, and wise women learn how to recognize them.

It is also important to choose friends who are willing to walk in agreement with godly values. This does not mean a friend must be perfect. It means there should be a shared respect for truth, character, and spiritual growth. When two people are walking in opposite directions, deep friendship becomes difficult and often painful.

Sometimes choosing wise friendships also means letting go of unhealthy ones. This can be hard, especially when you care deeply about someone. But peace, spiritual health, and obedience to God matter. The Lord is not asking you to be harsh. He is asking you to be wise.

Godly friendship is a blessing, but wisdom is the gatekeeper. When you ask the Lord for discernment, He will help you recognize who is safe, who is helpful, who is temporary, and who is not meant to walk closely with you. He knows how to protect your heart and lead you into relationships that honor Him.

Reflection Questions

1. Have you ever ignored warning signs in a friendship and later felt hurt?

____

____

____

2. What qualities do you believe make a friendship wise and healthy?

____

____

____

3. Are there relationships in your life that bring confusion, compromise, or emotional heaviness?

____

____

____

4. Do you tend to trust too quickly, or do you guard your heart too tightly?

____

____

____

5. How can discernment help protect your peace and your spiritual life?

____

____

____

6. What does it mean to love people without giving everyone close access to your heart?

____

____

____

7. Is God showing you any friendship that needs stronger boundaries or a different place in your life?

____

____

____

Prayer

Lord, thank You for caring about every area of my life, including my friendships. Give me wisdom and discernment in the relationships I choose. Help me to love people with kindness, but also to walk in truth and wisdom. Protect my heart from unhealthy connections, wrong influences, and relationships that pull me away from peace and from You. Teach me to recognize godly fruit, to pay attention to warning signs, and to trust Your guidance. Lead me into friendships that honor You and strengthen my walk with You. In Jesus' name, Amen.

Closing Encouragement

You do not have to feel guilty for choosing wisely. Loving others and using discernment can walk together. God never called you to give everyone the same access to your heart. He called you to be loving, but also wise.

When the Lord leads your friendships, He protects your peace and guides you toward relationships that are healthy, sincere, and life-giving.

Week 5:

The Blessing of Encouraging One Another

Theme

Godly friends strengthen one another with words, love, and faith.

Opening Thought

One of the sweetest blessings of friendship is encouragement. In a world that can be heavy, discouraging, and full of burdens, God often uses the presence and words of another person to bring strength to the weary heart. A godly friend does not merely share conversation—she brings comfort, hope, prayer, and life.

Many women are carrying silent battles. Some are smiling on the outside while fighting fear, grief, pressure, loneliness, or exhaustion on the inside. A kind word, a sincere prayer, a thoughtful message, or a faithful presence can become a lifeline in a difficult season. Encouragement may seem simple, but in God's hands, it becomes powerful.

The Lord never intended for His daughters to walk through hardship without support. He created friendship to be a place where hearts are strengthened, burdens are shared, and faith is stirred. When women encourage one another, they reflect the heart of Christ. They become vessels of comfort in a hurting world.

Encouragement is more than praise or flattery. True encouragement points the heart toward truth, hope, and God's faithfulness. It helps someone keep going when they feel weak. It lifts up instead of tearing down. It reminds the discouraged soul, *"You are not alone. God is with you. Keep trusting Him."*

Key Scriptures

1 Thessalonians 5:11
"Wherefore comfort yourselves together, and edify one another, even as also ye do."

Proverbs 27:9
"Ointment and perfume rejoice the heart: so doth the sweetness of a man's friend by hearty counsel."

Hebrews 3:13
"But exhort one another daily, while it is called To day; lest any of you be hardened through the deceitfulness of sin."

Lesson

Encouragement is a gift that strengthens the heart.

Godly friendship is not only about being present in good times. It is also about speaking life when someone feels weak, burdened, or discouraged. A true friend does not always have all the answers, but she offers something precious—love that strengthens and words that build up.

The Bible tells us to **comfort yourselves together** and **edify one another**. To edify means to build up. This means our words should not be careless, sharp, or destructive. They should be used to strengthen faith, bring peace, and remind others of God's truth. A godly woman understands that her words carry power. She can either bring healing or heaviness, courage or discouragement.

Encouragement is especially important because life is not easy. Women often carry many responsibilities and emotional burdens. Some are raising children, caring for family, working through grief, facing financial stress, healing from heartbreak, or fighting private battles no one else sees. In such seasons, a friend who encourages can become a source of refreshment.

Encouragement does not have to be grand to be meaningful. Sometimes it is a message that says, *"I am praying for you."* Sometimes it is a quiet reminder, *"God sees you."* Sometimes it is simply showing up, listening without judgment, or being present in someone's pain. Faithful encouragement often lives in small acts of love.

A godly friend also gives **hearty counsel**. This means she speaks from sincerity, wisdom, and love. She does not flatter just to please. She does not say empty words. She points her friend toward what is true, good, and helpful. Encouragement is not pretending everything is easy — it is helping someone remember that God is still faithful in the middle of difficulty.

There is also a healing power in mutual encouragement. We are not only called to receive it; we are also called to give it. Sometimes when we are struggling ourselves, God still uses us to strengthen someone else. Encouraging others can become part of our own healing, because it shifts our eyes back to the goodness and faithfulness of God.

The enemy loves discouragement because it makes people feel weak, isolated, and hopeless. But godly encouragement pushes back against that darkness. It brings light into heavy places. It reminds the heart not to give up. It helps women keep walking in faith.

You do not need to be a preacher, counselor, or leader to encourage someone. You simply need a heart yielded to God. He can use your words, your prayers, your kindness, and your presence to bless another woman more than you may ever know.

Reflection Questions

1. Has a friend ever encouraged you during a difficult season? What impact did it have on you?

____

____

____

2. What kind of words or actions make you feel strengthened and cared for?

____

____

____

3. Are your words usually life-giving and encouraging in your friendships?

____

____

____

4. Is there someone in your life right now who may need encouragement?

____

____

____

5. Do you tend to withhold encouraging words, or do you freely speak life into others?

____

____

____

6. How can you offer both kindness and truth when encouraging a friend?

____

____

____

7. What would it look like to make encouragement a regular part of your friendships?

____

____

____

Prayer

Lord, thank You for the gift of encouragement. Thank You for the people You place in our lives to strengthen us when we are weary. Help me to be a woman who speaks life, comfort, and truth. Guard my mouth from careless or discouraging words, and teach me to use my voice to build others up. Make me sensitive to those who are hurting, burdened, or quietly struggling. Let my words, prayers, and presence reflect Your love. Use me to bring hope to someone who needs strength today. In Jesus' name, Amen.

Closing Encouragement

Never underestimate the power of a kind word, a sincere prayer, or a faithful presence. God can use simple acts of encouragement to strengthen a weary soul. When you choose to build others up, you become a reflection of His heart.

A godly friend does not only stand beside others — she helps lift them up.

Week 6:

Friendship Through Difficult Seasons

Theme

True friendship remains present in seasons of pain, loss, and hardship.

Opening Thought

Friendship is easy in joyful seasons, but its depth is often revealed in difficult ones. When life is bright and everything feels steady, companionship may come naturally. But when sorrow enters, when prayers seem unanswered, when burdens grow heavy, or when the heart feels weary, that is when true friendship becomes especially precious.

Difficult seasons have a way of showing us what is real. They reveal who will stay, who will pray, who will listen, and who will lovingly walk beside us when life is not easy. A godly friend is not only someone who celebrates with us in times of blessing, but someone who stands with us in times of pain.

Many women know what it is to walk through grief, illness, disappointment, family struggles, heartbreak, betrayal, exhaustion, or spiritual battles. In such seasons, words may be few, tears may be many, and strength may feel small. Yet one faithful friend can become a gift from God—a source of comfort, presence, and compassion.

God never intended for us to face every hard season alone. He often ministers to us through the love, prayers, and presence of others. When friendship is rooted in Christ, it becomes a shelter in stormy times and a reminder that even in hardship, we are not abandoned.

Key Scriptures

Proverbs 17:17
"A friend loveth at all times, and a brother is born for adversity."

Romans 12:15
"Rejoice with them that do rejoice, and weep with them that weep."

Galatians 6:2
"Bear ye one another's burdens, and so fulfil the law of Christ."

Lesson

Godly friendship does not disappear when life becomes hard.

Anyone can be present when life is easy, but faithful friendship is proven in adversity. Proverbs tells us, *"A friend loveth at all times."* That means real friendship is not seasonal, convenient, or based only on happy circumstances. It is steady. It remains. It shows up when the heart is heavy and the road is hard.

Difficult seasons often make a woman feel vulnerable. Pain can leave her tired, quiet, and unsure of what she needs. Sometimes she may not have the words to explain what she is feeling. This is why the presence of a compassionate friend matters so deeply. A godly friend does not always need perfect words. Sometimes simply being there, listening, praying, and sitting in the silence is enough.

Romans 12:15 teaches us to *weep with them that weep.* This is a beautiful picture of compassion. It means we do not turn away from another person's pain because it feels uncomfortable. We do not rush them to heal, minimize their sorrow, or offer shallow answers. Instead, we enter that sorrow with tenderness. We make room for tears. We show mercy. We remind them that they do not have to carry their burden alone.

Bearing one another's burdens is part of Christlike love. Friendship is not only about laughter, shared interests, or pleasant moments. It is also about helping to carry the weight when someone feels overwhelmed. This may look like praying faithfully, offering help, checking in, listening patiently, or simply staying near when someone feels alone.

Difficult seasons can also test friendships. Some people pull away because they do not know how to handle pain. Others may grow impatient when sorrow lasts longer than they expected. But a godly friend understands that healing, grief, and hardship often take time. She does not rush the process. She gives grace for the season.

This kind of friendship reflects the heart of Jesus. Our Lord is near to the brokenhearted. He is compassionate, patient, and full of mercy. When we stand by others in difficult seasons, we reflect His love in a tangible way.

There may also be times when you are the one walking through hardship. In those moments, it is important to remember that needing support is not weakness. God often sends comfort through the people He places in our lives. Receiving love, prayer, and help from a trusted friend is part of His care for you.

Hard seasons may reveal pain, but they can also reveal the beauty of faithful friendship. The friends who stay close in adversity often become some of the greatest gifts we ever receive. Their love becomes a reminder that God sees us, cares for us, and has not left us alone.

Reflection Questions

1. Have you ever experienced a friendship that stayed with you during a difficult season?

____

____

____

2. How did that friend's presence or support affect your heart?

____

____

____

3. When someone is hurting, do you tend to lean in with compassion or pull back because you do not know what to say?

____

____

____

4. What does it mean to you to "bear ye one another's burdens"?

____

____

____

5. Are you currently walking through a hard season where
   you need support from a trusted friend?

____

____

____

6. Is there someone in your life right now who may need
   your compassion, prayers, or presence?

____

____

____

7. How can you reflect the heart of Christ in friendship
   during times of pain and adversity?

____

____

____

Prayer

Lord, thank You for being near to us in every difficult season. Thank You for the comfort and compassion You give when our hearts are heavy. Teach me to be a faithful friend who remains present in times of pain, loss, and hardship. Help me to love with patience, show compassion with sincerity, and carry the burdens of others with grace. And when I am the one who is hurting, help me to receive the care You provide through those You place around me. Let my friendships reflect Your mercy, Your tenderness, and Your steadfast love. In Jesus' name, Amen.

Closing Encouragement

Difficult seasons do not only reveal pain — they also reveal love that is real. A faithful friend is one who does not disappear when life grows heavy. She stays, she prays, she listens, and she loves.

When friendship is rooted in Christ, it becomes a beautiful reminder that even in hardship, you do not walk alone.

Week 7:

Healing from Friendship Wounds

Theme

God can heal the pain of broken, disappointing, and hurtful friendships.

Opening Thought

Friendship is one of God's beautiful gifts, but when friendship is wounded, the pain can run deep. Some hurts come from harsh words. Some come from betrayal, rejection, misunderstanding, abandonment, jealousy, or broken trust. Because friendship often involves love, closeness, and vulnerability, the wounds it leaves can be especially painful.

Many women carry silent pain from broken friendships. Some have been left out, talked about, used, rejected, or forgotten. Others opened their hearts, only to be hurt by someone they trusted. These wounds can leave lasting effects. They can make a woman fearful, guarded, insecure, or hesitant to trust again.

Friendship wounds are real, and they matter to God. He sees every tear, every disappointment, and every ache hidden behind a smile. He understands the sorrow of relational pain, and He does not ask us to ignore it. Instead, He invites us to bring it to Him so He can heal the places that hurt.

Healing does not mean pretending the wound never happened. It means allowing God to bring truth, comfort, cleansing, and restoration to the broken places of the heart. The Lord is able to heal what others damaged. He is able to restore peace where pain once lived. And He is able to teach us how to move forward without living imprisoned by past wounds.

Key Scriptures

Psalm 55:12–14
"For it was not an enemy that reproached me; then I could have borne it: neither was it he that hated me that did magnify himself against me; then I would have hid myself from him: But it was thou, a man mine equal, my guide, and mine acquaintance. We took sweet counsel together, and walked unto the house of God in company."

Psalm 34:18
"The Lord is nigh unto them that are of a broken heart; and saveth such as be of a contrite spirit."

Isaiah 41:10

"Fear thou not; for I am with thee: be not dismayed; for I am thy God: I will strengthen thee; yea, I will help thee; yea, I will uphold thee with the right hand of My righteousness."

Lesson

God cares about the wounds friendship can leave behind.

One of the hardest things about friendship pain is that it often comes from someone we trusted. Psalm 55 shows us the sorrow of being wounded not by an enemy, but by someone close. That kind of pain can feel confusing and deeply personal. It touches places of the heart that were opened in love and trust.

When friendship wounds are left untreated, they can harden the heart. A woman may begin to think, *I will never trust again. I will keep my distance. I do not want to be hurt anymore.* While those feelings are understandable, staying in that place too long can cause pain to shape the way we live. God does not want us to remain bound by bitterness, fear, or emotional walls.

Healing begins with honesty before God. We do not heal by pretending we are fine. We heal by bringing our pain into the presence of the Lord. We tell Him the truth about what hurt us. We tell Him where trust was broken, where rejection pierced us, where words wounded us, and where disappointment still lingers. God is not offended by honest tears. He welcomes them.

The Lord is near to the brokenhearted. He does not stand at a distance from your pain. He comes close to it. He comforts, strengthens, and upholds. He reminds you that what happened to you does not define your worth. Another person's betrayal does not change your value. Another person's rejection does not determine your identity. You are still loved, seen, and held by God.

Healing also involves surrender. Sometimes we replay the hurt over and over in our minds. We hold on to what was said, what was done, or what was lost. But God invites us to place that pain into His hands. Surrender does not excuse wrong. It simply means we stop carrying the wound as though we must heal ourselves. We let God become the healer of our hearts.

This healing may take time. Some wounds are deep. Some friendships affected important seasons of your life. Some losses still ache because they mattered. Be patient with your healing process. God is gentle with wounded hearts. He does not rush you, but He does walk with you.

Healing from friendship wounds also prepares the heart for wisdom. It teaches us discernment, healthy boundaries, and dependence on God. Over time, the Lord can turn even painful experiences into places of growth. He can make you wiser without making you hard, more discerning without making you bitter, and more careful without making you closed off from every future relationship.

You may not be able to change what happened, but with God's help, you do not have to remain trapped by it. The Lord is able to heal your heart and restore your peace.

Reflection Questions

1. Have you ever been deeply hurt in a friendship?

____

____

____

2. What kind of pain did that friendship wound leave in your heart?

____

____

____

3. Have those wounds made it harder for you to trust others?

____

____

____

4. Are there hurts you have tried to ignore instead of bringing to God?

____

____

____

5. What does it mean to you that the Lord is near to the brokenhearted?

____

____

____

6. Is there a wound you need to surrender to God for healing today?

____

____

____

7. How can God help you become wiser without becoming hard-hearted?

____

____

____

Prayer

Lord, You see every friendship wound I carry. You know every place where I have been hurt, disappointed, rejected, or betrayed. Thank You for being near to the brokenhearted. I bring my pain to You today and ask You to heal the wounded places in me. Remove bitterness, fear, and heaviness from my heart. Help me not to live guarded by pain, but guided by Your truth and peace. Strengthen me, comfort me, and restore what has been broken inside of me. Teach me how to move forward with wisdom, grace, and healing. In Jesus' name, Amen.

Closing Encouragement

Friendship wounds may be deep, but they are not beyond the healing touch of God. The Lord sees every hurt you carry, and He is able to restore peace to the places pain once occupied. What wounded you does not have the final word — God does.

He is near, He is gentle, and He is able to heal your heart.

Week 8:

Forgiveness and Grace in Friendship

Theme

Healthy friendship requires mercy, humility, and a heart willing to forgive.

Opening Thought

No friendship is perfect, because no person is perfect. Even in meaningful and godly relationships, there can be misunderstandings, disappointments, hurt feelings, careless words, and moments of weakness. This is why forgiveness and grace are so important in friendship. Without them, even good relationships can become strained, wounded, and broken.

Many women know the pain of being hurt by a friend. Sometimes the hurt is small but lingering. Sometimes it is deep and difficult to release. When pain is not brought to God, it can quietly grow into resentment, distance, or bitterness. A heart that once felt open and loving can become guarded and heavy.

Forgiveness does not mean pretending nothing happened. It does not mean calling wrong right. And it does not always mean every friendship will return to the same level of closeness. But forgiveness does mean choosing to release the offense into God's hands rather than allowing it to poison your heart.

Grace and forgiveness are part of the character of Christ. As women who have received mercy from God, we are also called to extend mercy to others. This can be difficult, especially when the wound is real, but the Lord never asks us to forgive in our own strength. He gives grace for what He commands.

Key Scriptures

Ephesians 4:31–32
"Let all bitterness, and wrath, and anger, and clamour, and evil speaking, be put away from you, with all malice: And be ye kind one to another, tenderhearted, forgiving one another, even as God for Christ's sake hath forgiven you."

Colossians 3:13
"Forbearing one another, and forgiving one another, if any man have a quarrel against any: even as Christ forgave you, so also do ye."

Matthew 6:14–15
"For if ye forgive men their trespasses, your heavenly Father will also forgive you: But if ye forgive not men their trespasses, neither will your Father forgive your trespasses."

Lesson

Forgiveness protects the heart from bitterness.

Friendship can be one of life's sweetest gifts, but it can also be a place where pain enters. Because friendship involves trust, honesty, and emotional closeness, offenses can cut deeply. A careless word, broken confidence, misunderstanding, or act of betrayal can leave the heart wounded. When these hurts are not dealt with in God's presence, they can begin to harden the heart.

That is why Scripture tells us to put away bitterness, wrath, anger, and evil speaking. Bitterness is dangerous because it does not stay small. It quietly grows. It affects the way we think, speak, and relate to others. It can make a woman suspicious, cold, or emotionally distant. God does not want His daughters to live with that kind of burden in their hearts.

Forgiveness is not first about the other person—it is also about the condition of your own heart before God. When you forgive, you are choosing not to let the offense rule you. You are releasing the weight of it into the hands of the Lord. You are saying, *"God, this hurt me, but I will not let this pain become bitterness in my soul."*

Grace is also necessary in friendship because people will fail. Even faithful friends can have moments of weakness. Sometimes offenses are intentional, and sometimes they are not. Sometimes hurt comes from immaturity, misunderstanding, or poor communication. Grace allows room for human weakness without ignoring truth. It helps us respond with tenderness, humility, and wisdom.

This does not mean forgiveness removes all boundaries. There are times when trust must be rebuilt slowly, and there are relationships that may not return to what they once were. Forgiveness and reconciliation are not always the same. Forgiveness can happen in the heart even when wisdom requires distance or change.

Forgiveness is often a process. A woman may need to bring the same hurt to God more than once. She may have to choose forgiveness again when the memory resurfaces. This does not mean she has failed. It means healing is unfolding. The Lord sees the sincerity of every step toward freedom.

When we remember how much mercy God has shown us, it softens our hearts toward others. We have all needed grace. We have all fallen short. We have all needed the kindness of the Lord. As we receive His mercy, He teaches us how to extend it to others.

Grace in friendship also means being quick to apologize when we are the one who caused hurt. A godly woman is not too proud to say, *"I was wrong."* Humility strengthens relationships. It opens the door for healing, peace, and restoration.

Forgiveness may feel costly, but bitterness costs more. Forgiveness opens the heart to peace. It makes room for God's healing to flow. It keeps pain from becoming poison. And it helps friendships reflect the mercy and love of Christ.

Reflection Questions

1. Is there a friendship hurt you are still carrying in your heart?

____

____

____

2. Have you found it difficult to forgive someone who wounded you?

____

____

____

3. What is the difference between forgiveness and pretending the hurt did not matter?

____

____

____

4. Has bitterness tried to grow in your heart because of a friendship wound?

____

____

____

5. Are there times when you have needed grace and
    forgiveness from others?

____

____

____

6. Is there someone you need to release into God's hands
    today?

____

____

____

7. How can forgiveness and grace make your heart freer and
    your friendships healthier?

____

____

____

Prayer

Lord, thank You for the mercy and forgiveness You have given to me. You know every hurt I carry from friendship, every offense that wounded me, and every place where bitterness has tried to grow. Help me to forgive as You have forgiven me. Give me grace to release pain into Your hands and not hold on to resentment. Teach me to walk in kindness, tenderness, and humility. And where I have caused hurt, help me to be honest, repentant, and willing to make things right. Let Your mercy shape my heart and bring peace where pain has lived. In Jesus' name, Amen.

Closing Encouragement

Forgiveness does not say the hurt was small. It says God is greater than the hurt. When you place an offense into His hands, you make room for peace, healing, and freedom. Grace keeps your heart soft, and forgiveness keeps your heart clean.

In friendship, mercy is not weakness — it is the beauty of Christ shining through you.

Week 9:
Setting Healthy Boundaries

Theme

Godly friendship is loving, but it is also wise.

Opening Thought

Healthy friendship is a gift from God, but even good relationships need wisdom. Many women have loving hearts and generous spirits, yet without healthy boundaries, friendship can become draining, confusing, or even harmful. Boundaries are not walls of bitterness—they are lines of wisdom that protect peace, honor truth, and help relationships remain healthy.

Some women struggle with boundaries because they do not want to seem unkind. Others fear rejection, so they say yes when they should say no. Some have been taught that love means unlimited access, endless giving, or never speaking up for themselves. But biblical love is not foolish, and godly friendship is not without wisdom.

Boundaries help protect the heart from unhealthy patterns. They teach us how to love others without losing peace, how to be kind without being controlled, and how to care without carrying what God never asked us to carry. Boundaries are not the absence of love—they are often the protection of it.

God does not call His daughters to live overwhelmed, manipulated, emotionally exhausted, or spiritually burdened by relationships that lack wisdom. He calls us to walk in both love and discernment. Healthy boundaries help us do that.

Key Scriptures

Proverbs 4:23
"Keep thy heart with all diligence; for out of it are the issues of life."

Matthew 10:16
"Behold, I send you forth as sheep in the midst of wolves: be ye therefore wise as serpents, and harmless as doves."

Galatians 6:5
"For every man shall bear his own burden."

Lesson

Boundaries protect the heart and help friendship remain healthy.

A boundary is a wise limit that protects what God has entrusted to you — your peace, your heart, your time, your emotional well-being, and your spiritual health. Without boundaries, even friendship can become a place of confusion, pressure, and imbalance. Godly friendship should bring encouragement and peace, not constant heaviness and disorder.

Proverbs tells us to **keep thy heart with all diligence**. That means guarding it carefully. This does not mean becoming cold, suspicious, or closed off from everyone. It means being prayerful and wise about what you allow into the inner places of your life. Not every person should have the same level of access to your heart, your time, or your trust.

Jesus Himself showed both love and wisdom. He was compassionate, merciful, and available, yet He also walked in discernment. He did not entrust Himself to every person. He knew when to withdraw, when to speak, when to remain silent, and when to set limits. If our Lord walked with boundaries, then boundaries cannot be unloving.

Many women struggle because they confuse being loving with being endlessly available. They feel guilty for saying no. They feel responsible for fixing everyone's problems. They may tolerate disrespect, over giving, or emotional pressure because they do not want to hurt anyone's feelings. But love without wisdom can lead to exhaustion.

Galatians reminds us that **every man shall bear his own burden**. This teaches us that while we are called to care for one another, we are not called to carry what belongs to someone else. There is a difference between supporting a friend and becoming responsible for her choices, emotions, or unhealthy patterns. A boundary helps you know where your responsibility ends and another person's begins.

Healthy boundaries may look like:
saying no without guilt,
limiting time with someone who brings constant chaos,
refusing to participate in gossip,
protecting private matters,
speaking honestly when something is hurtful,
or stepping back from a relationship that is manipulative or harmful.

Boundaries are especially important when a friendship becomes one-sided. If one person is always giving and the other is always taking, the relationship can become imbalanced. A healthy friendship has mutual respect. It does not demand unlimited access or use guilt to control. A godly friend will honor your peace, respect your limits, and value honesty.

Setting boundaries does not mean you do not love someone. It means you are choosing to love with wisdom. Sometimes a boundary is what keeps a relationship from becoming bitter, resentful, or unhealthy. Clear limits can actually protect friendship and make space for more honesty and peace.

There may also be times when boundaries are necessary because a relationship is unsafe or deeply damaging. In those cases, wisdom is not cruelty. Stepping back, limiting access, or ending close contact may be the healthiest choice. God does not call you to stay in places that continually harm your heart and disturb your peace.

A boundary spoken with humility and truth is not selfish. It is stewardship. God has entrusted you with your heart, your mind, and your peace. Protecting them with wisdom honors Him.

Reflection Questions

1. What comes to your mind when you hear the word **boundaries**?

____

____

____

2. Do you find it difficult to say no or set limits in friendship?

____

____

____

3. Have you ever felt emotionally drained because a relationship lacked healthy boundaries?

____

____

____

4. Are there places in your life where you have allowed too
    much access to your heart or peace?

____

____

____

5. What is the difference between being loving and being
    controlled?

____

____

____

6. Is God showing you a boundary that needs to be set or
    strengthened?

____

____

____

7. How can boundaries help your friendships become
    healthier and more peaceful?

____

____

____

Prayer

Lord, thank You for caring about my peace, my heart, and my relationships. Teach me how to love others with both kindness and wisdom. Help me to set healthy boundaries without fear, guilt, or hardness. Show me where I have overextended myself, ignored warning signs, or allowed unhealthy patterns to continue. Give me courage to say no when needed, to guard my heart with diligence, and to walk in discernment. Let my boundaries reflect Your truth, Your peace, and Your wisdom. In Jesus' name, Amen.

Closing Encouragement

Boundaries are not a sign that you love less. They are often a sign that you are learning to love wisely. God never asked you to abandon peace in order to keep people comfortable. He called you to walk in truth, wisdom, and grace.

A healthy boundary can protect your heart and preserve the beauty of godly friendship.

Week 10:

Friendship in the Body of Christ

Theme

Sisterhood in Christ is a gift from God, and we are called to strengthen one another in faith.

Opening Thought 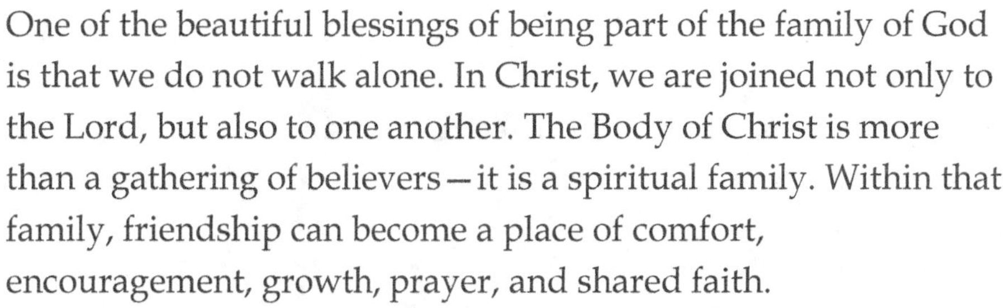

One of the beautiful blessings of being part of the family of God is that we do not walk alone. In Christ, we are joined not only to the Lord, but also to one another. The Body of Christ is more than a gathering of believers — it is a spiritual family. Within that family, friendship can become a place of comfort, encouragement, growth, prayer, and shared faith.

Christian friendship carries something precious because it is rooted in more than personality, convenience, or common interests. It is rooted in Christ. When women walk together in the Lord, their friendship can become a source of strength through every season. They can pray for one another, sharpen one another, carry one another's burdens, and remind each other of God's truth.

Yet even within the church, friendship can sometimes be misunderstood, neglected, or wounded by comparison, division, or unmet expectations. That is why God's Word calls us to unity, care, and mutual honor. He did not design His daughters to compete, isolate, or wound one another, but to walk together in love.

Sisterhood in Christ is not about perfection. It is about belonging to the same Savior, growing under the same grace, and learning to love one another as members of one body. When women in the Body of Christ walk in humility, kindness, and faithfulness, friendship becomes a testimony of God's love.

Key Scriptures

Romans 12:4–5
"For as we have many members in one body, and all members have not the same office: So we, being many, are one body in Christ, and every one members one of another."

1 Corinthians 12:25–27
"That there should be no schism in the body; but that the members should have the same care one for another. And whether one member suffer, all the members suffer with it; or one member be honoured, all the members rejoice with it. Now ye are the body of Christ, and members in particular."

Psalm 133:1

"Behold, how good and how pleasant it is for brethren to dwell together in unity!"

Lesson

Friendship in the Body of Christ should reflect the love and unity of Jesus.

When a woman comes into the family of God, she is not only given a relationship with the Lord—she is also placed among spiritual brothers and sisters. This is part of God's wisdom and goodness. He knows we need fellowship, encouragement, and the support of others who share our faith.

Christian friendship is powerful because it can strengthen the soul in ways that ordinary companionship cannot. A sister in Christ can pray with you when your heart is burdened. She can speak Scripture over you when your faith feels weak. She can rejoice with you in God's blessings and stand with you when you are going through sorrow. Friendship in the Body of Christ is meant to reflect the care of Jesus through His people.

Romans reminds us that we are **members one of another**. This means our lives are connected. We are not called to live as isolated believers, each carrying our burdens in silence. We are called to care for one another, support one another, and grow together in faith. God designed the Body to function with love, unity, and mutual dependence.

This kind of friendship requires humility. In the church, it can be easy for comparison, insecurity, or misunderstanding to create distance between women. One woman may feel overlooked, while another may feel inadequate. Sometimes differences in age, personality, gifting, or life season can make women feel disconnected. But God never intended these differences to divide us. Instead, He calls us to honor one another and remember that every woman has value in His kingdom.

The Body of Christ is strongest when there is no schism, no unnecessary division, and no spirit of competition. A godly friendship in the church should not be marked by jealousy, exclusion, gossip, or hidden bitterness. It should be marked by love, prayer, respect, and sincere care. A mature woman of God does not tear down another sister — she strengthens her.

Friendship in the Body of Christ also means learning to rejoice and grieve together. Scripture says if one member suffers, all suffer with it, and if one is honored, all rejoice with it. This is a beautiful picture of genuine sisterhood. It means we do not become jealous when another woman is blessed. We celebrate her. It also means we do not ignore a sister's pain. We make room for it and stand with her in love.

Unity does not mean everyone is the same. It means we are joined by something greater than our differences: Jesus Christ. In Him, we can walk together with grace. We can build one another up instead of competing. We can be safe places for one another in a world that is often cold and divided.

Sometimes women long deeply for this kind of Christian friendship and have not yet experienced it in the way they hope.

If that is true for you, do not lose heart. Keep asking God to plant you among faithful women who love Him and love others well. He knows how to connect hearts in His time.

As the Body of Christ walks in unity, friendship becomes more than companionship — it becomes ministry. It becomes a living expression of God's care.

Reflection Questions

1. What does it mean to you to be part of the Body of Christ?

____

____

____

2. Have you experienced friendship in the church that strengthened your faith?

____

____

____

3. Are there ways comparison or insecurity have affected your relationships with other Christian women?

____

____

____

4. How can you help build unity rather than division among
    women in the Body of Christ?

____

____

____

5. Do you find it easy to rejoice when another woman is
    honored or blessed?

____

____

____

6. Is there a sister in Christ who may need your
    encouragement, prayer, or friendship in this season?

____

____

____

7. What kind of Christian friendship are you asking God to
    build in your life?

____

____

____

Prayer

Lord, thank You for placing me in the Body of Christ and for the gift of spiritual family. Help me to walk in unity, humility, and love with my sisters in Christ. Remove comparison, jealousy, insecurity, and anything that would cause division in my heart. Teach me to care for others sincerely, to rejoice with those who rejoice, and to weep with those who weep. Make me a woman who strengthens the Body, honors other women, and reflects the love of Jesus in friendship. Lead me into godly sisterhood that brings You glory. In Jesus' name, Amen.

Closing Encouragement

You were not meant to follow Christ alone. God has placed you in His family, and within that family, there is beauty in godly sisterhood. As women walk together in humility, love, and unity, they reveal the heart of Jesus to one another.

Friendship in the Body of Christ is more than fellowship — it is a gift of grace.

Week 11:

Reaching Out and Building Meaningful Connection

Theme

Meaningful friendship often begins with courage, openness, and a willing heart.

Opening Thought

Many women long for meaningful connection, yet reaching for it can feel difficult. Sometimes the heart desires friendship, but fear, past wounds, insecurity, shyness, or disappointment make it hard to take the first step. A woman may want deeper connection, yet still hesitate to open her heart because she does not want to be misunderstood, rejected, or hurt again.

This is a tender and very real struggle. Longing for friendship and fearing it at the same time can leave a woman feeling torn inside. She may pray for connection, but still find herself holding back. She may want to reach out, but question whether she will be welcomed. She may deeply desire sisterhood, yet feel unsure where to begin.

But meaningful connection often requires courage. It often begins with one small step — one conversation, one invitation, one message, one moment of openness, one choice to try again. Building friendship does not always happen instantly. It is often formed gently, over time, through sincerity, faith, and trust.

God understands the fears that can make reaching out feel hard. He sees every lonely place, every guarded place, and every quiet longing for connection. He is able to strengthen the heart and give courage for new beginnings. When we place our fears in His hands, He helps us move forward with wisdom, grace, and hope.

Key Scriptures

Isaiah 43:1–2
"But now thus saith the Lord who created thee, O Jacob, and He that formed thee, O Israel: "Fear not, for I have redeemed thee; I have called thee by thy name; thou art Mine. When thou passest through the waters, I will be with thee; and through the rivers, they shall not overflow thee. When thou walkest through the fire, thou shalt not be burned, neither shall the flame kindle upon thee."

2 Timothy 1:7
"For God hath not given us the spirit of fear; but of power, and of love, and of a sound mind."

Philippians 4:6–7

"Be careful for nothing; but in every thing by prayer and supplication with thanksgiving let your requests be made known unto God. And the peace of God, which passeth all understanding, shall keep your hearts and minds through Christ Jesus."

Lesson

God gives courage for meaningful connection.

Many women wait for friendship to come to them, yet sometimes God invites us to participate in the answer to our own prayer. Reaching out can feel vulnerable, but vulnerability is often part of how connection begins. This does not mean we throw our hearts open without wisdom. It means we allow God to help us take healthy, prayerful steps toward meaningful relationships.

Fear is one of the greatest obstacles to connection. Fear of rejection. Fear of not fitting in. Fear of being overlooked. Fear of being hurt again. These fears can quietly keep a woman isolated, even when she longs for friendship. But Scripture reminds us that God has not given us the spirit of fear. Fear may speak loudly, but it is not the voice that should lead us.

God gives power, love, and a sound mind. He gives courage to the hesitant heart. He gives peace to the anxious mind. He gives wisdom to help us know when to step forward and when to move slowly. When we bring our fears to Him in prayer, He strengthens us to move in faith instead of being ruled by fear.

Building meaningful connection often begins with simple acts. It may be introducing yourself to another woman at church, joining a Bible study, sending a kind message, asking someone to have coffee, checking on someone who seems alone, or choosing to stay after service and speak instead of quietly leaving. Small steps can open doors to beautiful relationships.

Meaningful connection also requires sincerity. Deep friendship is not built on pretending, performing, or trying to impress others. It grows where there is honesty, kindness, and openness. You do not have to become someone else to be loved. You do not have to strive for perfection to be worthy of connection. The right people will value the grace of God in you, not a polished image.

There may be times when reaching out does not lead to immediate closeness. Not every effort will become a deep friendship, and that is okay. Building connection takes time, patience, and prayer. Some relationships remain casual, while others grow slowly into something deeper. Do not despise small beginnings. God often builds beautiful things little by little.

It is also important to remember that loneliness is not always solved by being around more people. Meaningful connection is built through safe, sincere, Christ-centered relationships. This is why we must reach out with both courage and discernment. We do not force connection, but we do remain open to what God may be building.

If past wounds have made your heart guarded, be gentle with yourself. Healing and courage often grow together. You may not be ready to trust quickly, and that is all right. Ask God to help you take one healthy step at a time. He knows how to restore confidence where hurt once lived.

The Lord is able to bring meaningful connection into your life, but He may also ask you to partner with Him by stepping out of isolation. One kind word, one invitation, one conversation, or one act of courage may become the beginning of something beautiful.

Reflection Questions

1. Do you find it easy or difficult to reach out and build new friendships?

____

____

____

2. What fears have made meaningful connection feel hard for you?

____

____

____

3. Have past hurts made you hesitant to open your heart again?

____

____

____

4. What small step of courage might God be asking you to take in this season?

____

____

____

5. How can prayer help calm your fears about friendship and connection?

____

____

____

6. Are there places where you have been waiting for connection, but God may be inviting you to reach out?

____

____

____

7. What does meaningful, Christ-centered connection look like to you in this season of life?

____

____

____

Prayer

Lord, You know the desire of my heart for meaningful connection, and You also know the fears that can make reaching out feel difficult. Thank You that You have not given me the spirit of fear, but of power, and of love, and of a sound mind. Help me to trust You with my heart and to take wise, healthy steps toward the relationships You may be preparing for me. Heal every place in me that still feels afraid, rejected, or guarded. Give me courage to reach out, grace to be sincere, and peace to rest in Your guidance. Lead me into meaningful, Christ-centered connection in Your perfect way and timing. In Jesus' name, Amen.

Closing Encouragement

Meaningful connection often begins with one brave step. You do not have to force friendship or strive to be someone you are not. Simply place your heart in God's hands, and let Him lead you with wisdom and peace.

The Lord who sees your longing is also able to guide your steps toward the connection your heart has been praying for.

Week 12:

The Beauty of Lasting Godly Friendship

Theme

Friendships rooted in Christ can become lasting gifts of love, strength, and faithfulness.

Opening Thought

Some friendships are brief and seasonal, while others become lasting treasures. There is something deeply beautiful about a friendship that endures through time, prayer, trials, growth, and changing seasons. Lasting godly friendship is not built merely on shared interests or convenience. It is built on love, faithfulness, trust, grace, and a foundation in Christ.

Many women long for this kind of friendship—a relationship marked by sincerity, loyalty, encouragement, and spiritual depth. They long for a friend who will remain through both joy and sorrow, who will pray with them, rejoice with them, and continue walking beside them as life changes. This kind of friendship is precious because it reflects something of the steadfast love of God.

Lasting friendship does not mean perfect friendship. Even strong relationships will face misunderstandings, distance, busy seasons, and moments that require grace. But when friendship is rooted in Christ, it has a strength that can endure those things. It is held together not only by affection, but by shared faith, humility, forgiveness, and mutual care.

The beauty of lasting friendship is that it becomes a place of rest in a restless world. It becomes a reminder that faithful love still exists, that God still joins hearts, and that meaningful connection is possible. A lasting godly friend is truly a gift.

Key Scriptures

Ecclesiastes 4:9–12
"Two are better than one; because they have a good reward for their labour. For if they fall, the one will lift up his fellow: but woe to him that is alone when he falleth; for he hath not another to help him up. Again, if two lie together, then they have heat: but how can one be warm alone? And if one prevail against him, two shall withstand him; and a threefold cord is not quickly broken."

Ruth 1:16–17
"And Ruth said, Intreat me not to leave thee, or to return from following after thee: for whither thou goest, I will go; and where thou

lodgest, I will lodge: thy people shall be my people, and thy God my God..."

1 Thessalonians 5:11
"Wherefore comfort yourselves together, and edify one another, even as also ye do."

Lesson

Lasting friendship is a gift strengthened by faithfulness and grace.

One of the reasons lasting godly friendship is so beautiful is because it is not easily shaken. It has weathered real life. It has been tested by time, hardship, distance, and change—and yet it remains. This kind of friendship does not happen by accident. It is nurtured through faithfulness, patience, prayer, and mutual care.

Ecclesiastes reminds us that **two are better than one** and that a **threefold cord is not quickly broken**. When God is in the center of a friendship, that relationship gains deeper strength. It is no longer built only on emotion or circumstance. It is anchored in something eternal. Christ becomes the One who helps hold hearts together through changing seasons.

The friendship of Ruth and Naomi gives us a beautiful picture of loyalty. Ruth's words reveal commitment, devotion, and steadfast love. She did not remain only when life was easy. She stayed in uncertainty, grief, and transition. Lasting friendship often carries this kind of faithfulness. It says, *"I will not walk away simply because the season has become hard."*

This kind of friendship is rare, but it is real. It is found in hearts that are willing to love beyond convenience. It is built through shared prayers, honest conversations, acts of kindness, forgiveness, and a mutual desire to honor God. Lasting friendships do not remain strong because problems never arise; they remain strong because grace, humility, and love help carry them through.

A lasting godly friend becomes a blessing in many ways. She encourages you when your faith is weak. She celebrates God's goodness in your life without jealousy. She speaks truth with love. She remembers your burdens. She prays for you. She becomes part of your story — not as someone temporary, but as someone whose faithfulness leaves a lasting mark.

It is also important to understand that lasting friendship is not measured only by constant closeness or daily conversation. Life changes. Seasons shift. Responsibilities grow. Sometimes faithful friends may not speak every day, yet the bond remains rooted in love, prayer, and sincerity. Time and distance do not destroy what God has built deeply.

If you have been blessed with even one lasting godly friend, thank the Lord for that gift. If you are still longing for that kind of friendship, do not lose heart. God knows how to join hearts in beautiful ways. He is able to bring into your life women who will walk with you in faith, grace, and truth.

Lasting friendship is also something we help cultivate. It grows where there is faithfulness, encouragement, honesty, grace, and shared commitment. It deepens when both hearts are willing to invest, forgive, communicate, and pray. A strong friendship is not only found — it is also nurtured.

As this study comes to a close, remember this: meaningful connection is not beyond your reach. God is able to heal wounds, teach wisdom, strengthen character, and build beautiful friendships in His time. The beauty of lasting godly friendship is not just in having someone beside you — it is in seeing the faithfulness of God reflected through a relationship that endures.

Reflection Questions

1. What qualities do you believe make a friendship lasting and strong?

2. Have you experienced a friendship that remained faithful through changing seasons?

3. What does the phrase **a threefold cord is not quickly broken** mean to you in friendship?

____

____

____

4. In what ways can you help cultivate lasting, healthy friendship in your own life?

____

____

____

5. Are there friendships in your life that you need to cherish more intentionally?

____

____

____

6. If you long for lasting godly friendship, what hope does this lesson give you?

____

____

____

7. How have these twelve weeks changed the way you view friendship?

____

____

____

Prayer

Lord, thank You for the gift of godly friendship and for the beauty of relationships rooted in You. Thank You for every faithful friend You have placed in my life, and for the love, encouragement, and strength that friendship can bring. Help me to be a woman who values, nurtures, and protects godly friendship with grace and faithfulness. Teach me to love well, forgive quickly, encourage sincerely, and remain rooted in Christ. And if there are still places in my heart longing for deeper connection, I place those desires into Your hands. Trusting that You are able to bring beautiful and lasting friendship in Your perfect time. In Jesus' name, Amen.

Closing Encouragement

Lasting godly friendship is one of Heaven's sweetest gifts. When friendship is rooted in Christ, strengthened by grace, and held together by faithfulness, it becomes a beautiful reflection of God's love.

What God builds with truth, love, and grace can become a lasting blessing for the heart.

Closing Encouragement

As you come to the end of **The Gift of Godly Friendship**, I pray your heart has been strengthened, comforted, and reminded of God's beautiful design for meaningful connection.

Friendship is one of the precious gifts the Lord gives to His daughters. Through this study, we have seen that godly friendship is not built on perfection, popularity, or convenience. It is built on Christ. It is shaped by love, wisdom, faithfulness, grace, forgiveness, encouragement, and truth. It is nurtured in humility and protected by discernment. It is strengthened through prayer and sustained by the hand of God.

Perhaps as you walked through these pages, the Lord revealed places of longing in your heart. Perhaps He reminded you of the beauty of true friendship, the importance of wisdom, the need for healing, or the courage it takes to open your heart again. Perhaps He showed you wounds that still need His touch, or friendships that need more grace, more prayer, or more intention. Whatever He has revealed, know this: **He is faithful to continue the work He has begun in you.**

If you have been blessed with godly friendships, thank the Lord for them and cherish them well. If you are still longing for deeper, Christ-centered connection, do not lose heart. The God who created you for relationship understands that longing. He sees every quiet prayer, every lonely place, and every hope hidden in your heart. He knows how to bring the right people into your life in the right season.

Never believe the lie that meaningful friendship is beyond your reach. God is able to build what pain tried to break. He is able to heal what disappointment wounded. He is able to guide you with wisdom, protect your heart with truth, and lead you into connections that reflect His love.

As you move forward, continue to seek friendship God's way. Stay rooted in your friendship with Him. Let His Word guide your heart. Let His Spirit shape your character. Let His wisdom guard your relationships. And let His love flow through you as you encourage, strengthen, forgive, and walk in grace with others.

May you become the kind of woman whose presence brings peace, whose words bring life, whose heart carries wisdom, and whose friendships reflect the beauty of Jesus Christ.

And may the Lord bless you with friendships that are sincere, healing, faithful, and filled with His love.

Final Scripture

"Two are better than one; because they have a good reward for their labour. For if they fall, the one will lift up his fellow..."

Ecclesiastes 4:9–10

Final Prayer

Lord, thank You for walking with me through this journey of learning about godly friendship. Thank You for every truth You have planted in my heart, every wound You are healing, and every place where You are teaching me to love with wisdom and grace. Continue to shape me into a woman who reflects Your heart in friendship. Lead me into relationships that honor You and strengthen my faith. Heal every lonely place, restore every wounded place, and fill my life with Your peace and presence. Thank You that I am never alone, because You are with me. In Jesus' name, Amen.

About the Author

Dr. Lende Click is a Christian author, counselor, and Bible teacher devoted to helping women find healing, hope, and renewed strength in the presence of God. Through her inspiring books, devotionals, and Bible studies, she writes with tenderness, biblical truth, and spiritual insight—encouraging readers to trust God in every season and embrace the beauty of His restoring love.

Her work is marked by compassion, faith, and a deep desire to see lives transformed by the power of God's Word. With a heart for the broken and a passion for uplifting women, Dr. Click's writing speaks to those who are seeking peace, purpose, and meaningful connection with Christ.

She is a **NCCA Licensed Professional Clinical Counselor, Certified Temperament Counselor, NCCA Licensed Clinical Pastoral Counselor, NCCA Licensed Christian Counselor,** and holds advanced certifications in **Death and Grief Therapy** and **Integrated Marriage and Family Therapy.** She is also a member of the **American Association of Christian Counselors (AACC)** and the **National Christian Counselors Association (NCCA).**

From **Augusta, Georgia,** Dr. Click continues to write with a mission to bring healing to wounded hearts, encouragement to weary souls, and glory to the Lord through every page.

www.ingramcontent.com/pod-product-compliance
Lightning Source LLC
Chambersburg PA
CBHW051133160726
47997CB00019B/2352